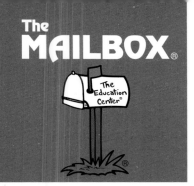

The MAILBOX®

W9-CEZ-359

Circus

THE BEST OF The MAILBOX® MAGAZINE

Our best circus activities and reproducibles from the 1998–2004 issues of *The Mailbox®* and *Teacher's Helper®* magazines

- **Phonological-Awareness Ideas**

- **Phonics Activities**

- **Writing Activities**

- **Math Activities**

- **Learning Centers**

- **Arts-and-Crafts Ideas**

Build Core Skills!

And Much More!

Editorial Team: Becky S. Andrews, Kimberley Bruck, Diane Badden, Thad H. McLaurin, Sharon Murphy, Karen A. Brudnak, Juli Docimo Blair, Sarah Hamblet, Hope Rodgers, Dorothy C. McKinney

Production Team: Lori Z. Henry, Pam Crane, Rebecca Saunders, Chris Curry, Sarah Foreman, Theresa Lewis Goode, Greg D. Rieves, Eliseo De Jesus Santos II, Barry Slate, Donna K. Teal, Zane Williard, Tazmen Carlisle, Kathy Coop, Marsha Heim, Lynette Dickerson, Mark Rainey, Karen Brewer Grossman

www.themailbox.com

©2007 The Mailbox®
All rights reserved.
ISBN10 #1-56234-743-8 • ISBN13 #978-156234-743-7

Except as provided for herein, no part of this publication may be reproduced or transmitted in any form or by any means, electronic or mechanical, including photocopying, recording, or storing in any information storage and retrieval system or electronic online bulletin board, without prior written permission from The Education Center, Inc. Permission is given to the original purchaser to reproduce patterns and reproducibles for individual classroom use only and not for resale or distribution. Reproduction for an entire school or school system is prohibited. Please direct written inquiries to The Education Center, Inc., P.O. Box 9753, Greensboro, NC 27429-0753. The Education Center®, *The Mailbox*®, the mailbox/post/grass logo, and The Mailbox Book Company® are registered trademarks of The Education Center, Inc. All other brand or product names are trademarks or registered trademarks of their respective companies.

Manufactured in the United States
10 9 8 7 6 5 4 3 2 1

Table of Contents

Thematic Units

Build a variety of developmentally appropriate skills with even more circus ideas and activities.

Reinforce basic skills with fun, ready-to-use practice pages and patterns.

UNDER THE BIG TOP

Where's the greatest place on earth to find shapes? At "The Greatest Show on Earth"—the circus! The following high-flying circus activities will have your youngsters shaped up on shapes. So come on everyone! Let's join the circus!

ideas contributed by LeeAnn Collins

sorting by shape

I SPY

Challenge your little ones to spy all the different shapes at the circus with this center idea. In advance, use a photocopier to make copies of the patterns on page 6. Color the patterns. Laminate them and then cut out each one. Set the patterns in the center along with three embroidery hoops to represent circus rings. Or use lengths of yarn to create the rings. Invite each child to find the shape in each pattern and then sort the patterns into the rings by shape.

matching basic shapes

WALKING A TIGHTROPE

The tightrope walkers at the circus are always a popular act. So invite your youngsters to practice shape recognition by walking a simple tightrope. In advance, place lines of masking tape on the floor of your circle time area. Then tape construction paper shapes to each line of tape as shown. Next, cut out paper shapes to match those on the floor and then place them in a paper bag. To begin the activity, have a child pull a shape out of the bag, find the matching shapes on the floor, and then walk heel-to-toe across the line of tape between them. Continue the activity in this manner until each child has had a turn to walk a tightrope.

HERE COMES THE CIRCUS TRAIN

All aboard! What better way to reinforce shapes than to have youngsters create this circus train! To prepare, use the patterns on page 7 to create a supply of animal cutouts. Provide each child with a sheet of construction paper and two black paper circles. Have the child create a train car by gluing the black circles to the paper as shown. Invite the child to choose an animal cutout and glue it onto the car. Then direct him to color the animal and draw the shape of his choice around it.

When each child has completed a car, tape a train engine cutout to a wall and attach the cars to the engine. Gather your group around the train and invite each child to identify some shapes on it.

BUNCHES OF BALLOONS

At the circus, balloons are abundant! At this center, size-seriation skills and shape discrimination will balloon! To prepare, cut out a set of felt ovals in a variety of sizes. Hot-glue a length of yarn to each oval to create a pretend balloon. Place the felt balloons near your flannelboard and invite each child to line up the balloons from smallest to largest. For an added challenge, add a set of circular balloons to the oval balloons. Have students sort the balloons by shape and then arrange each set by size.

PRETEND PIE TOSS

Every clown knows that a pie in the face is just part of the job! Invite your students to join in some lighthearted circus fun with this small-group activity. To prepare, create construction paper clown faces similar to the ones shown or use the patterns on pages 33 and 36. Laminate the faces and then use double-sided tape to attach them to a wall. Next, cut out circle shapes from sponges to make pretend pies. Place the sponges a short distance away from the clowns. Invite a small group of children to the area. Have a child toss the "pie" at the clowns and then identify the shape of the clown that was hit (or nearly hit). Repeat the pie practice with a different child. Any way you toss it, this activity is sure to be a hit!

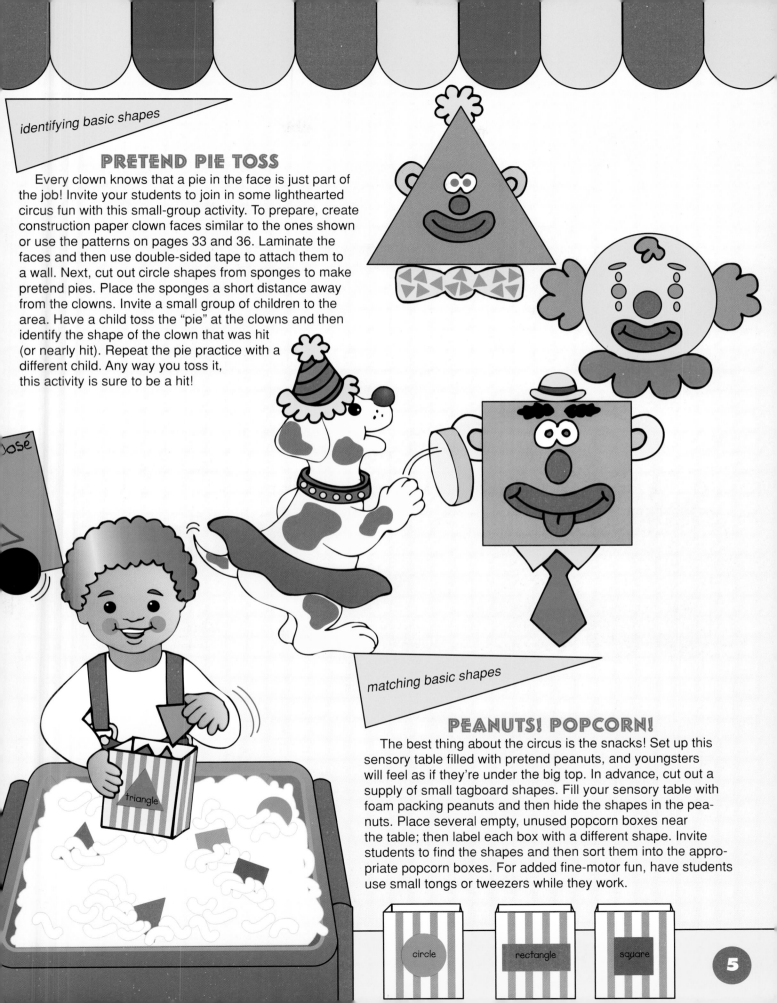

PEANUTS! POPCORN!

The best thing about the circus is the snacks! Set up this sensory table filled with pretend peanuts, and youngsters will feel as if they're under the big top. In advance, cut out a supply of small tagboard shapes. Fill your sensory table with foam packing peanuts and then hide the shapes in the peanuts. Place several empty, unused popcorn boxes near the table; then label each box with a different shape. Invite students to find the shapes and then sort them into the appropriate popcorn boxes. For added fine-motor fun, have students use small tongs or tweezers while they work.

Circus Patterns
Use with "I Spy" on page 3.

TEC61057

popcorn

TICKET to the CIRCUS

©The Mailbox® • Circus • TEC61057

©The Mailbox® • *Circus* • TEC61057

Name _____

Colorful Clown

Color by the code.

Color Code

○ –red

☐ –blue

△ –yellow

▭ –orange

©The Mailbox® • Circus • TEC61057

Sizin' Up Shapes

Read.

✔ the correct boxes.

The shape has	square ⬜	rectangle ▭	triangle △	circle ◯
corners				
sides				
3 corners				
straight sides				
3 sides				
4 corners				
4 sides				

Look at the ✔.

✏️Write.

Which shape has only 3 corners and 3 sides? _____

Which shape is round? _____

Name

Poppin' Shapes

Color by the code.

Color Code

⬡ —purple

△ —red

▭ —blue

▱ —green

©The Mailbox® • *Circus* • TEC61057

Clowning Around
With Patterns

Looking and listening for patterns is a big stepping-stone in making math (as well as science, music, art, and language) make sense. So let these kooky clowns present patterns to your youngsters in a way that is friendly and fun.

Strike a Pose
Creating and extending patterns of poses

Use these clown cards to get your students into the act! To prepare, make four tagboard copies of page 14; then color the clowns and cut the cards apart. Working with a small group, have a student volunteer pick two of the cards. Then help several children arrange themselves into an ABAB pattern that mimics the clown poses on the cards. Challenge the rest of the students to join in and pose accordingly to extend the pattern. Continue in this manner using different clown cards and different patterns, such as AABAAB, ABBABB, and AABBAABB. And for the final act? Use three clown cards!

Carrie Richardson and Betty Horton
Dr. S. A. Mudd Elementary School, Waldorf, MD

Sounds Like a Pattern!
Identifying and repeating sound patterns

Clowns and their antics are not only a sight for the eyes but are also a feast for the ears! Enlist a clown's collection of sound effects to help your little ones with patterning. Gather an assortment of objects and instruments that make clown-related sounds, such as a slide whistle, a bike horn, a cowbell, cymbals, and wood blocks.

Use two of the objects to create a sound pattern; then encourage a student volunteer to recreate the pattern. To make the activity more challenging, perform the pattern out of children's view or prerecord the sounds. Honk, honk, crash! Honk, honk, crash!

A Shoe Show
Creating shoe patterns

Looking for another way to create more patterns? Look no further than your feet! Have your youngsters create these shoes to clown around in and then use the shoes for some patterning fun. Gather the materials listed below. Then encourage each child to paint the backs of two paper plates. (Make sure the child uses only one color.) When the paint is dry, cut a wedge from each plate and punch a hole at each corner. Help the child knot a length of yarn through each hole. Then tie the plates around the child's ankles to create clown shoes.

Once all of the children are wearing their silly shoes, encourage them to arrange themselves into patterns according to the shoe colors. Let's see, blue, blue, red, red...What a shoe show!

Sheila Crawford
Kids Kampus
Huntington, IN

Materials needed:
2 thin paper plates
(per child)
four 12" pieces of yarn
(per child)
paint (2 or 3 colors)
in tubs
paintbrushes
scissors
hole puncher

Fanciful Flowers
Identifying and repeating a color pattern

This patterning activity puts your clown theme in full bloom. Use a black marker to draw simple clown hats across several sentence strips as shown. Draw a green stem coming from each hat. Then use a flower-shaped sponge to make prints in different colors, creating a unique pattern on each strip. Place the strips in the art center, along with the flower sponge, paints, and a supply of longer paper strips (from a cash register roll). Encourage each child to visit the center, choose a hat strip, and then replicate and extend its pattern on her paper strip. Hats off to patterns!

adapted from an idea by Carrie Richardson and Betty Horton
Dr. S. A. Mudd Elementary School
Waldorf, MD

Juggling Jamboree
Creating color patterns with objects and with representations

Any time there are clowns, there has to be some juggling! Invite your little jesters to demonstrate their talents with an assortment of sponge or rubber balls. Then put the balls in the math center for some patterning practice. You'll also need to include three empty sterilized egg cartons to keep the balls from rolling away. In the center, have each child turn the egg cartons over so that the egg cup portions are facing upward. Then direct him to align the balls between the cups to create a pattern as shown. If desired, provide strips of paper and bingo bottle markers (in the same colors as the balls) for children to use to recreate and extend their patterns.

Stacie Stone Davis, Lima, NY

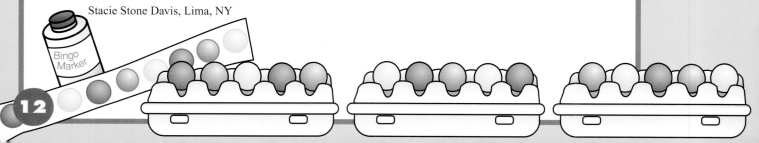

Up, Up, and Away
Translating from one pattern representation to another

Patterning will become a popular activity when you use these cute clowns. To prepare, make six copies of the clown pattern on page 15. Color, cut out, and then laminate the clowns. Cut out a supply of balloon patterns on page 16 from red, blue, green, and yellow construction paper. Tape a length of string to the back of each balloon before displaying the clowns and a pattern of six balloons on a bulletin board. Make a booklet for each child by cutting a sheet of paper into four strips, stacking the strips, and stapling them together on the left side. Each child will also need a supply of colored sticky dots (to match the balloon patterns).

During circle time, direct youngsters' attention to the clowns. Have a student volunteer read the pattern. Then have each student record and repeat the color pattern in his booklet using sticky dots to resemble balloons and squiggly lines to resemble strings. Change the balloon pattern each of the next three days and repeat the activity. After four days, put the balloons and clowns in a center and continue to vary the patterns for more patterning practice.

Stacie Stone Davis
Lima, NY

Be a Clown
Creating and repeating patterns of movements

Clowns are just full of activity! Have youngsters brainstorm all the different ways clowns move, such as throwing pies, waving hello, tipping their hats, and dancing. List students' responses on chart paper. Explain that patterns exist not only in objects and sounds, but also in movements. Write a simple pattern on the board, such as AABB. Designate a movement from the chart for A and a different movement for B. With lots of exaggeration, have a group of students make the sequence of movements represented by the pattern. Continue with different patterns, actions, and children until everyone has had a turn. What funny, funny clowns!

Stacie Stone Davis

The Final Act
Creating and extending shape patterns

Have your youngsters create this cast of clowns to display their improved knowledge of patterns. Gather the materials listed below. Then use the directions that follow to help each child make her own clown. Mount all of the completed projects on a bulletin board titled "Patterned Pranksters." Clowns, clowns, clowns!

Materials needed for each clown:

9" paper plate	shape stickers or cutouts
half of a 1½" foam ball	red permanent marker
half of a 10" paper doily	craft glue
tagboard triangle with one 8" side	markers
pom-pom	

Directions:
1. Use the red permanent marker to color the rounded side of the foam ball half.
2. Use markers to create the clown's eyes, cheeks, mouth, and hair on the back side of the paper plate.
3. Glue the red nose to the plate to finish the clown's face.
4. Glue the doily half to the underside of the plate so that its edges show, creating the clown's collar.
5. Make a pattern with the shape stickers along the bottom edge (the eight-inch side) of the triangle hat.
6. Glue the pom-pom to the tip of the hat.
7. Glue the hat to the clown's head.

adapted from ideas by Stacie Stone Davis, Lima , NY, and Sheli Gossett, Sebring, FL

Clown Cards

Use with "Strike a Pose" on page 11.

TEC61057

TEC61057

TEC61057

TEC61057

TEC61057

TEC61057

©The Mailbox® • Circus • TEC61057

TEC61057

Balloon Patterns
Use with "Up, Up, and Away" on page 13.

©The Mailbox® • *Circus* • TEC61057

Clowning Around With Nouns

Ladies and gentlemen…and children of all ages! Welcome to the greatest part of speech of them all—nouns!

What Is a Noun?

Introduce your youngsters to the wide world of **nouns** by sharing *A Mink, a Fink, a Skating Rink: What Is a Noun?* by Brian P. Cleary. This read-aloud's clever rhymes will help students identify nouns and see that they are, indeed, everywhere. Follow up by teaching students the nifty little song (right), sung to the tune of "I'm a Little Teapot."

Vicki Dabrowka
Concord Hill School
Chevy Chase, MD

What Is a Noun?
A noun is a fine word.
Yes sirree!
A person, a place,
Or an object you see.
Can you paint a picture of the word?
If you can, it's a noun you've heard!

A Rainbow of Nouns

Add a splash of color to your study of **nouns**, and create a striking word bank for students to use in their creative writing! First, divide children into six groups, and assign each group a color of the rainbow: red, orange, yellow, green, blue, or violet (purple). Have each group brainstorm and name nouns that are its assigned color while a recorder lists them on a sheet of paper. After you check each list for spelling, provide each group with construction paper in its assigned color. Instruct the children in each group to trace hand shapes on their paper, label each shape with a noun from the list, and then cut out all of the shapes. Use these cut-outs to create a rainbow of nouns on a bulletin board or wall space. A pot of gold… filled to the brim with nouns!

adapted from an idea
by Erin Harp
Manchester, NJ

Particularly Proper Nouns

Creative writing, spelling, capitalizing, and building vocabulary—they're all packed into this activity that helps youngsters understand and use **proper nouns**. Each morning, write a list of five common nouns on the board. Make sure these common nouns are ones for which youngsters can easily name matching proper nouns. Have each child copy the list onto her own paper. Then, beside each common noun, instruct her to write a proper noun that matches it. Continue this activity for several days by mixing and matching the common nouns that you write on the board.

Linda Masternak Justice
Kansas City, Missouri

Have a Seat!

Review **singular and plural nouns** with this versatile game! First, program a class set of index cards with singular nouns. Also number another set of index cards, one per child, and tape each card to a chair. (Make a duplicate of one number card—without revealing it to students—and place it in an envelope.) Arrange the chairs in a circle in any order; then invite students to stand with you in a circle, one student at each chair.

To play, display a singular-noun card to the first child in the circle. The child reads the word on the card, spells its plural form, and then uses the plural in a sentence. If he is correct, he chooses a chair and sits down. If he's incorrect, put the card on the bottom of the deck and go to the next student. Continue playing until every student is seated. Then open the envelope and reveal the hidden number. The student sitting in the chair with the matching number is the winner!

Sara Harris, West View Elementary, Knoxville, TN

Up, Up, and Away!

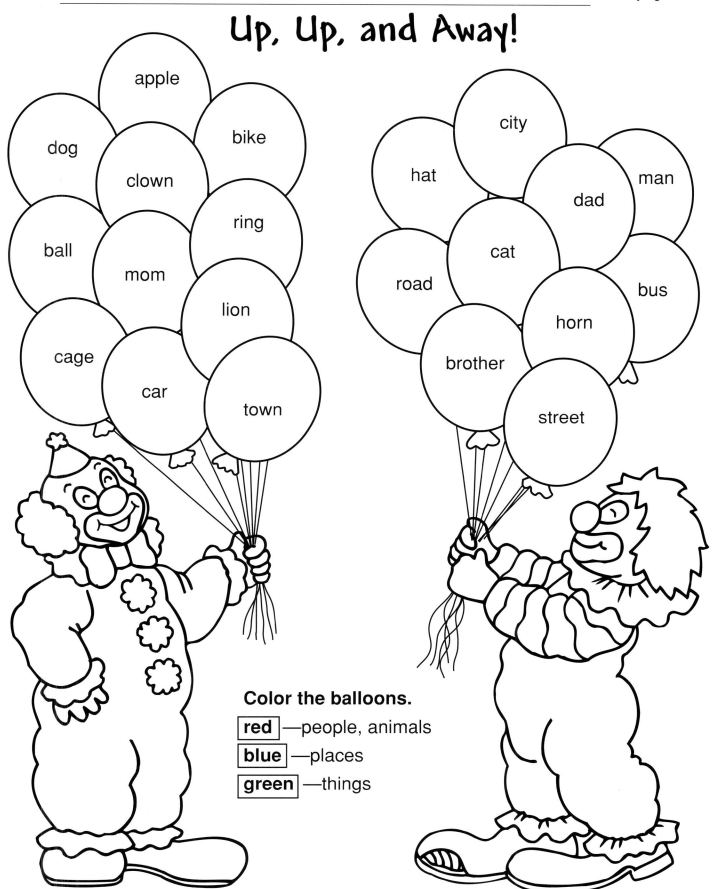

apple
dog
bike
clown
ball
ring
mom
cage
lion
car
town

city
hat
man
dad
road
cat
bus
horn
brother
street

Color the balloons.

red —people, animals
blue —places
green —things

Name

Clown Nouns

✏️ Add **s** to each word.

🖍️ Draw a picture to show more than one.

dog

bear

lion

ball

hat

wagon

car

©The Mailbox® • *Circus* • TEC61057

Pattern Blocks Under the Big Top

Looking for a kid-pleasing way to reinforce math skills? Pattern blocks will do the trick!

Juggling Shapes
Naming, making, and extending patterns

This pattern-making idea puts a colorful spin on teamwork! Divide students into groups of three or four and give each youngster a blank card. Provide a marker, sentence strip, and container of pattern blocks for each group. Ask the group members to place their sentence strip on the floor and sit in a row facing it.

To begin, the first child in each group writes on her card a three- or four-element pattern sequence, such as ABAC. She announces the sequence and places the card above the sentence strip. To begin the pattern, she sets a pattern block on the left end of the sentence strip. Students take turns adding blocks to the sentence strip to establish the pattern. They extend the pattern to include a designated number of repetitions and then they read the pattern to check their work. Next, they clear away the pattern blocks, and a different child begins another pattern. The group continues in this manner until every child has a turn beginning a pattern. To provide additional practice, place a sentence strip, the student-programmed cards, and a supply of pattern blocks at a center and have students create labeled illustrations of the patterns they make.

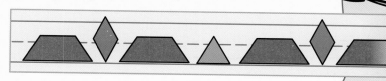

adapted from an idea by Kelly Hanover
Vernon Elementary School
Kenosha, WI

Computation by Design
Solving addition and subtraction problems

Shape up computation skills with this partner activity! Each twosome needs a supply of pattern blocks and two sheets of paper. Partner 1 uses pattern blocks in two or three different shapes to make a figure. Partner 2 counts each set of shapes. Then he writes and solves the corresponding addition problem. Partner 1 counts the pattern blocks to check his partner's work. The partners switch roles and repeat the activity as time allows.

To modify the idea for subtraction practice, Partner 1 makes a pattern block figure. Partner 2 writes the total number of blocks used. Then Partner 1 removes a desired number of pattern blocks, concealing them from his partner. Partner 2 counts the remaining pattern blocks and subtracts this number from the total. Partner 1 reveals the pattern blocks he removed to check the difference.

Searching for Symmetry
Recognizing and creating symmetrical shapes

Line up this activity to set students' sights on symmetry! Confirm that students understand that a figure has *line symmetry* if it can be divided into two parts that match exactly. Then provide time for each youngster to experiment with pattern blocks to make symmetrical figures. To ensure that a figure is symmetrical, instruct her to hold a pencil over it to look for lines of symmetry and then make any needed adjustments.

For an eye-catching follow-up, have each child glue pattern block cutouts (patterns on page 23) onto provided construction paper to re-create her favorite symmetrical figure. For each line of symmetry, ask her to glue a length of yarn in place. Display students' work on a bulletin board titled "Setting Our Sights on Symmetry!"

adapted from an idea by Jeannine Perez, Sky City Community School, Pueblo of Acoma, NM

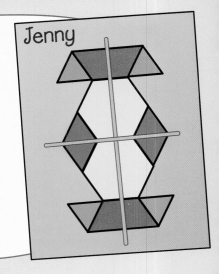

Shapely Instructions
Naming shapes and relative positions

This idea provides practice with giving precise (and shapely!) instructions. Give each student an identical set of pattern blocks. Pair students and ask each youngster to sit facing his partner. Instruct partners to stand a folder between them so that each youngster's pattern blocks are hidden from his partner's view. Partner 1 uses four to six pattern blocks to make a figure. Next, he uses position and shape words to direct his partner to make an identical figure. The partners remove the folder and compare their work. Then they switch roles and repeat the activity. Now that's a nifty way to put geometry skills in place!

Sheila Criqui-Kelley, Lebo Elementary, Lebo, KS

Priceless Figures
Exploring money amounts

Looking for a way to boost money skills? Pattern blocks are a wise investment! Display the provided code and then cash in on one or more of the following ideas.

"Cent-sational" Shapes: A student visually divides her paper into quarters. In each section, she glues two pattern block cutouts (or traces two pattern blocks). Below each pair of shapes, she writes an addition sentence to show the total value.

Costly Comparisons: Pair students. Each partner randomly selects two pattern blocks and then determines the combined value. The partners write their totals and use the appropriate math sign to compare them. They repeat the activity a specified number of times.

They're Equal: Place pattern blocks and several cards labeled with coin amounts at a center. Arrange for students to visit the center in pairs. One partner selects a card. Each partner makes a pattern block figure that represents the corresponding value. The partners discuss any differences in the blocks they chose and the equivalent coin amounts. Then they continue with the remaining cards.

See page 23 for pattern block cutouts.

Code

triangle	= 1¢
rhombus	= 5¢
trapezoid	= 10¢
hexagon	= 25¢

5¢ + 10¢ = 15¢   5¢ + 5¢ = 10¢

25¢ + 10¢ = 35¢   1¢ + 10¢ = 11¢

Michele Daughenbaugh
Park Forest Elementary
State College, PA

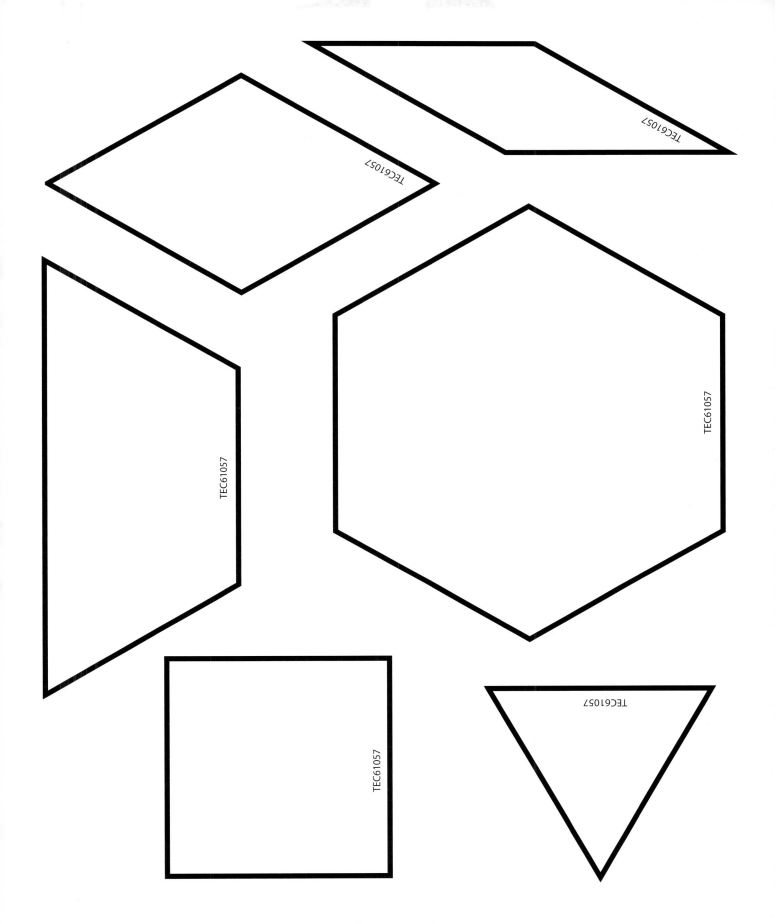

TEC61057

TEC61057

TEC61057

TEC61057

TEC61057

TEC61057

©The Mailbox® • *Circus* • TEC61057

Note to the teacher: Copy and cut out a construction paper supply of these pattern blocks to use with the ideas on pages 21 and 22.

23

Taking Shape

Part 1

Fill in the two figures with pattern blocks.
Trace the pattern blocks. Color.

Part 2

Follow the directions to fill in the figures below.
Then trace the pattern blocks. Color.

| Use 3 different shapes. | Use 6 of the same shape. |

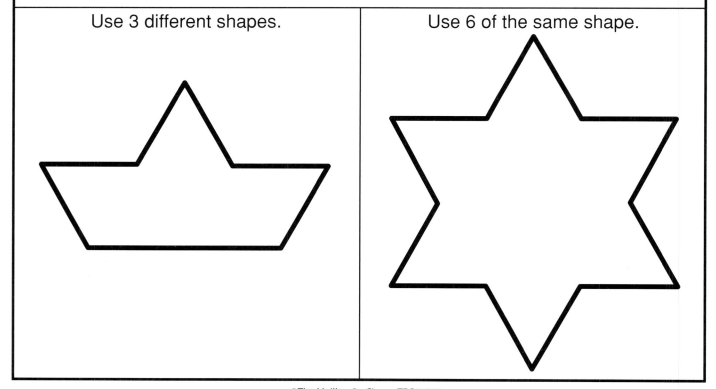

Note to the teacher: To complete this activity, each student needs a supply of pattern blocks.

More Circus Ideas

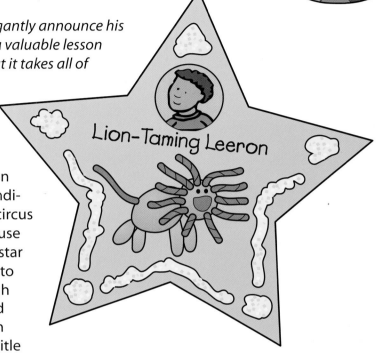

Star of the Circus

By Michael and Mary Beth Sampson
Illustrated by Jose Aruego and Ariane Dewey

One animal after another claims center ring to arrogantly announce his status as "Star of the Circus." But the performers learn a valuable lesson about cooperation and respect when they discover that it takes all of them to create a star circus.

Highlight your students' fantasies of big-top fame with this star-studded **literature** idea. After reading and discussing this story, give each child a yellow construction paper copy of the star pattern on page 34. Help him cut out his star and the circle as indicated. Label the star with the child's self-appointed circus name, such as "Lion-Taming Leeron." Have the child use crayons, glitter pens, and craft items to decorate his star to correspond with his circus title. Then glue his photo to the back of the star so that the face shows through the circle. Later, invite each child to share his star and a sample of his star performance with the class. Then display the stars on a big-top background with the title "Now Starring..."

Funny Faces

This grin-inducing partner game will have students clowning around with **long *a* vowels**! Give each student a copy of the game cards on page 35 and the game pieces on page 36 (for larger cards and pieces, duplicate the pages at 125% onto 11" x 17" paper). To make her game, a student colors the game pieces; then she cuts out the pieces and cards. She stores her game in a large resealable plastic bag. To play, one student in each pair shuffles her cards and stacks them face-down on a playing surface. Each student, in turn, draws a card and reads the word. If it has a long *a* sound, she selects one facial feature and places it on her clown face. Then she places the card in a discard pile. If the word has a short *a* sound, she places the card in a discard pile and her turn is over. The first player to complete a clown face that consists of two eyebrows, two eyes, one nose, and one mouth wins. (Have students shuffle the discarded game cards and restack them as needed.)

Sara Harris
West View Elementary
Knoxville, TN

Clown Colors

Reinforce **color words** with this cute booklet! Duplicate the reproducible on page 37 on white construction paper to make a booklet cover for each student. (To make back covers, duplicate the outline on any color of construction paper.) To make the booklet's pages, duplicate one copy of the outline per child for each color that you wish to include in the booklets. Have each student cut out her covers and pages before stapling them together to make a booklet. Provide a model for students to write a color word on each page of their booklets. Have the students illustrate each page by drawing pictures of their choice in the appropriate color.

Clancey Clown's Bag

To prepare for this **letter-sound** activity, glue paper cutouts of the letters *C* and *c* to a brown paper bag. Fill the bag with a variety of small objects, making sure that you have several that begin with *c* (for example, cork, candy, cotton, corn, cookie, caboose, camera, candle, can, cap, car, etc.). Empty the bag's contents onto a table. Have students decide which objects from the collection should be placed in Clancey Clown's bag. Change the letters on the bag and repeat the activity to practice other initial consonants.

You will learn lots of cool stuff in science.

You will like Mrs. Goldsmith. She is funny!

A "Seal" of Approval

Your youngsters will have a ball helping to create a colorful **writing** display for your next class of students! First, invite students to share their fondest memories of the school year. Then have each child write a few positive words to the upcoming class on a blank card. Next, have each child color and cut out a beach ball pattern (page 38) and then glue his card in the center of his cutout. Collect the projects. Explain that the projects will be displayed on a bulletin board at the start of the next school year and invite the students to drop in and see their work. In the fall, title a bulletin board "Last Year's Students Give Their 'Seal' of Approval!" and showcase a seal balancing the students' colorful projects.

Caryl Goldsmith
John Hancock School
Philadelphia, PA

One-of-a-Kind Clowns

Do you believe that clowning around can enhance **descriptive writing**? You will at the conclusion of this activity! Have each child complete a copy of page 39. Encourage him to color his clown creatively and list two descriptive words for each clown part. Then provide plenty of time for students to write their sentences. For a fun follow-up, collect the students' completed papers. Tape the clown portraits to the board and then read the sentences to the class. Ask a different child to match each description to a clown.

Susan M. Stires
Sam Houston Elementary
Wichita Falls, TX

My Silly Clown
My clown has curly orange hair and two pink ears. His yellow nose is big and round. He is grinning because he just drank a big glass of milk. His hat is purple. It has circles on it.

Circus Critters

Looking to strengthen **descriptive-writing** skills? This circus-related project is sure to do the trick! Write a list of student-suggested circus animals on the board. Have each child secretly select one animal from the list and then, without revealing the animal's identity, write a description of it on a 2" x 9" strip of yellow construction paper. Next, she folds a 9" x 12" sheet of white construction paper in half (to 6" x 9"). Keeping the fold at the top, she partially unfolds the paper and illustrates the animal she described. She uses crayons to decorate the front of the folded paper to resemble an old-fashioned circus wagon. Then she glues her description to the top edge of the wagon (trimming it as desired) and two construction paper wheels to the bottom edge. For an interactive display, showcase the projects with the title "The Circus Is in Town!" Challenge students to read each description, decide which animal is described, and then peek inside the project to check her answer.

Doris Hautala
Washington Elementary School
Ely, MN

My animal is gray. It has four legs. Its ears are big! It has a very long trunk. It has a short tail.

Circus Shapes

Shape up youngsters' circus savvy with these creative collages. Divide youngsters into small groups. Provide each group with an assortment of shape tracers, brightly colored construction paper, and decorative gift wrap. Invite students to trace and cut out a variety of **shapes**. Then instruct each group to form a circus collage by cooperatively gluing their shapes onto a sheet of black bulletin board paper. Invite each group to tell about its collage; then display the completed works for all to see.

Polka-Dot Bow Ties

Make ten copies of the bow tie pattern (page 40)onto different colors of construction paper. Laminate the construction paper; then cut out the bow ties. With a permanent marker, write a numeral from 1 to 10 on the center of each of the bow ties. Place the patterns at a learning center with a zippered bag of counters. Have a student choose a bow tie, read the numeral, and place the correct number of polka dots on the bow tie. To change a numeral on a bow tie, spray the existing numeral with hair spray and it will wipe right off. Write a new numeral in the center of the bow tie with a permanent marker.

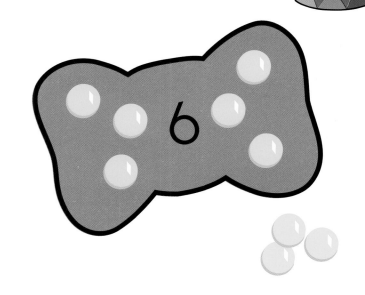

Clown Snacks

For this **estimating** activity, fill three identical, transparent containers with varying amounts of circus peanuts. Fill the jars so that the amount of circus peanuts can be easily visually distinguished. Ask children which jar has the most and which has the least amount of circus peanuts. Isolate one of the jars; then ask students to find a jar that has more than (or less than) the jar shown. Have groups of children work together to guess the number of circus peanuts in each jar. Write each group's guess on a chart; then count the circus peanuts together.

Ticket Lengths, Please!

A length of tickets admits each student to this **nonstandard-measurement** event! In advance, purchase a roll of tickets (or make copies of the patterns on page 41). Give each student a strip of five tickets. To prepare a recording sheet, each youngster divides a sheet of drawing paper into two columns. He labels the first column "Item" and the second column "Length."

Next, each student measures to the nearest whole ticket several classroom objects of various lengths. He writes each item and length on his paper. After he records several measurements, he identifies one item that is shorter than his strip of tickets and measures it to the nearest whole ticket. He tears off any extra tickets and discards them. He glues the strip of tickets in the middle of the blank side of his paper. Above the strip, he illustrates the item to show its actual length. Below the strip, he writes a sentence to tell the item's length in tickets. The result will be just the ticket to check students' use of nonstandard measurement!

This pencil is about 3 tickets long.

Kyle

Send in the Clowns!

Reinforce **addition** with the help of this crafty clown! To make one clown, cover a flip-top box with white paper (Maxwell House® filter pack coffee boxes work well). Cut a hole in the side of the box, through the paper. Add a large pom-pom nose, wiggle eyes, a scalloped collar, and yarn for hair. Place the clown in a center along with a laminated sheet of addition problems, a dry-erase marker, and a supply of manipulatives, such as wrapped pieces of candy. Invite each student to visit the center and use the clown and manipulatives to solve the equations. For example, to solve the equation $3 + 5$, the child places three candy pieces and then five candy pieces into the clown's mouth. He opens the lid of the box, counts the total number of pieces, and then uses the marker to write his answer on the sheet. When the child completes all of the equations, reward him with a tasty treat of his own. Erase his answers from the sheet; then invite another youngster to visit the center and feed the clown.

Gina Friederich, Remsen-Union Elementary, Remsen, IA

At the Gate

For this **patterning** activity, cut out different colored copies of the tickets on page 41 and place them in a basket. To play, have each of two students pretend to pay for a ticket and then draw one from the basket, making sure that two different colors are drawn. Instruct the youngsters to stand in front of the group and show their tickets to the class. Talk about the pattern that could be made using the two colors. Then, in turn, invite a student to choose an appropriate color of ticket to continue the pattern. For more practice, have students return the tickets to the basket and then repeat the activity to make a different pattern.

Hot Diggity Dog!

Here's a **patterning** activity that will have youngsters begging for a turn! Cut out construction paper copies of the hot dog patterns on page 42. Also cut a supply of three-inch lengths of yellow, red, and green yarn (mustard, ketchup, and relish). Have each child line up the hot dogs and then add yarn condiments, creating a pattern. One hot dog with mustard and relish, please!

Five Funny Circus Clowns

Have a few class clowns? Ask five children to volunteer to act out this poem; then transform them into clowns by putting one red sticky dot on each child's nose. Here come five funny circus clowns!

Here come five funny circus clowns
Doing their tricks while marching into town.
One is short and circles around.
One is bouncy and jumps up and down.
One is tall and stands so proud.
One is happy and waves at the crowd.
One is small and sweet and wee—
The funniest one you'll ever see.

LeeAnn Collins
Sunshine House Preschool, Lansing, MI

Create a Clown

Lots of giggles and grins are sure to come with this **art project**. Duplicate the clown face pattern below for each child. Glue the pattern inside a white paper plate. Then provide a wide variety of materials such as crayons, markers, buttons, construction paper, fabric scraps, yarn, curling ribbon, colored cellophane, colored clay, cereal pieces, colored or natural pasta, and cake-decorating toppings. Have children use these materials, glue, and lots of imagination to create their own original clowns. When they're dry, mount each finished clown on a bulletin board. Beneath each project, post a sentence that the child has dictated to you about his clown.

Clown Face Pattern

TEC61057

Star Pattern

Use with *Star of the Circus* on page 25.

Cut this out.

TEC61057

©The Mailbox® • *Circus* • TEC61057

ball TEC61057	vase TEC61057
way TEC61057	apple TEC61057
fan TEC61057	ape TEC61057
gray TEC61057	cave TEC61057
mad TEC61057	bag TEC61057
play TEC61057	hat TEC61057
cake TEC61057	cap TEC61057
whale TEC61057	glass TEC61057
skate TEC61057	jam TEC61057
rake TEC61057	add TEC61057

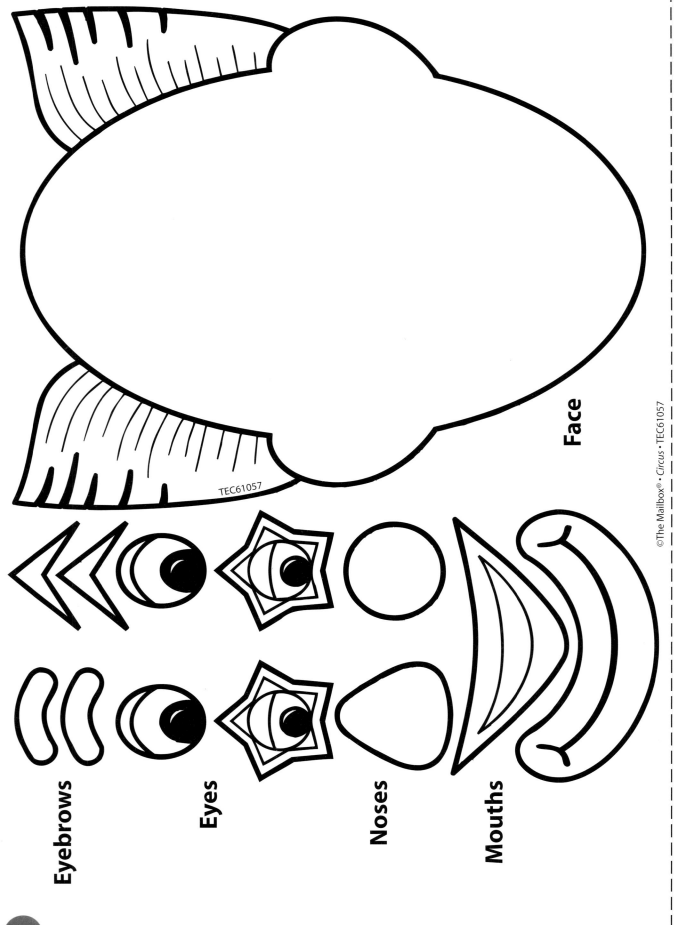

Face

Eyebrows

Eyes

Noses

Mouths

TEC61057

36

©The Mailbox® • *Circus* • TEC61057

Note to the teacher: Use with "Funny Faces" on page 25.

Shape Booklet Page

©The Mailbox® • *Circus* • TEC61057

Note to the teacher: Use with "Clown Colors" on page 26.

Beach Ball Pattern

Use with "A 'Seal' of Approval" on page 27.

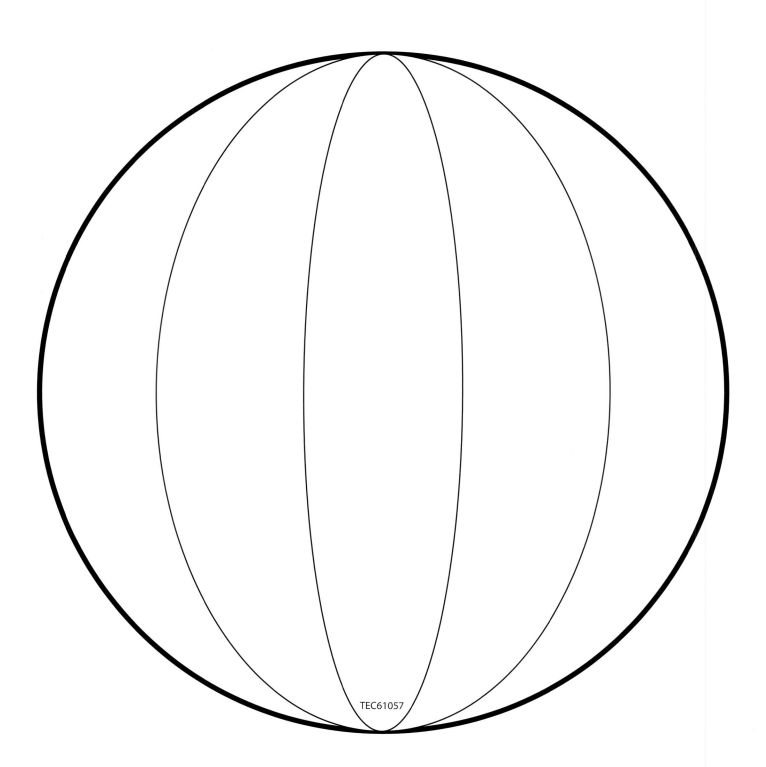

TEC61057

©The Mailbox® • *Circus* • TEC61057

Name _____

A One-of-a-Kind Clown

Color the clown.
Study each clown part listed below.
On the lines write words that tell about it.

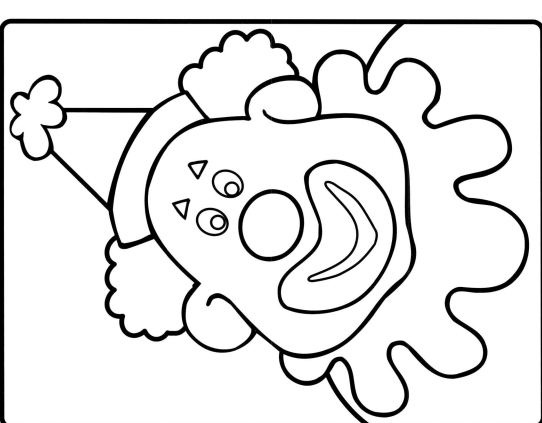

hat _____

hair _____

nose _____

ears _____

mouth _____

Use a sheet of writing paper.
Write sentences that describe the clown.
Be sure to use some of the words you listed!

©The Mailbox® • *Circus* • TEC61057

Note to the teacher: *Use with "One-of-a-Kind Clowns" on page 27.*

Bow Tie Pattern
Use with "Polka-Dot Bow Ties" on page 29.

TEC61057

©The Mailbox® • *Circus* • TEC61057

TICKET TEC61057 TICKET TEC61057 TICKET TEC61057 TICKET TEC61057 TICKET TEC61057 TICKET TEC61057 TICKET TEC61057

TICKET TEC61057 TICKET TEC61057 TICKET TEC61057 TICKET TEC61057 TICKET TEC61057 TICKET TEC61057 TICKET TEC61057

TICKET TEC61057 TICKET TEC61057 TICKET TEC61057 TICKET TEC61057 TICKET TEC61057 TICKET TEC61057 TICKET TEC61057

TICKET TEC61057 TICKET TEC61057 TICKET TEC61057 TICKET TEC61057 TICKET TEC61057 TICKET TEC61057 TICKET TEC61057

TICKET TEC61057 TICKET TEC61057 TICKET TEC61057 TICKET TEC61057 TICKET TEC61057 TICKET TEC61057 TICKET TEC61057

Hot Dog Patterns

Use with "Hot Diggity Dog!" on page 31.

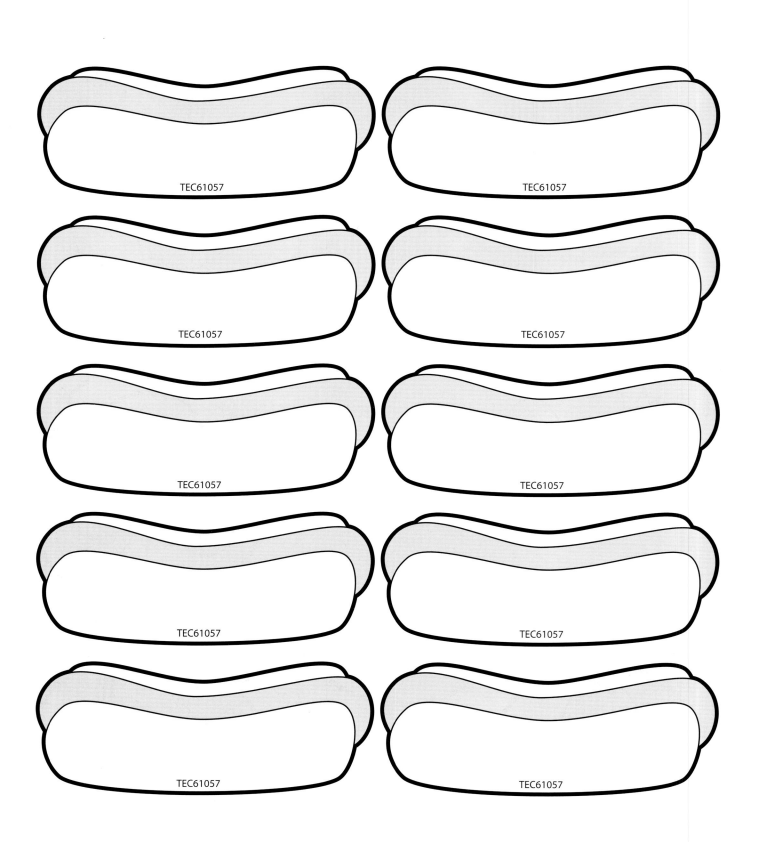

TEC61057

TEC61057

TEC61057

TEC61057

TEC61057

TEC61057

TEC61057

TEC61057

TEC61057

TEC61057

©The Mailbox® • *Circus* • TEC61057

Balancing Bear

Color the rhyming pictures the same color on each ball.

Performing for Peanuts

Cut. Match the rhyming pictures.

Glue.

©The Mailbox® • Circus • TEC61057

     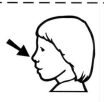

Name _____

Circus Juggler

Draw a line to match rhyming words.

Color each rhyming pair the same color.

bat

bell

duck

fox

pig

top

shell

box

wig

cat

mop

truck

Circus Stars

Color the picture if the beginning letter matches.

©The Mailbox® • Circus • TEC61057

Spectacular Endings

Name each picture and say its ending sound.
Write the ending letter.
Color each box as you go.

r	s	t	n	g	p	m	d	x

fo _____

wi _____

ha _____

ca _____

gu _____

bu _____

ca _____

be _____

cu _____

©The Mailbox® • Circus • TEC61057

47

Treats for the Clowns

Estimate. Then use paper clips to measure.
Answer the questions.

Estimate. about _____ paper clips   Measure. about _____ paper clips

Tiny

Estimate. about _____ paper clips   Measure. about _____ paper clips

Penny

Estimate. about _____ paper clips   Measure. about _____ paper clips

Curly

Estimate. about _____ paper clips   Measure. about _____ paper clips

Pal

1. Which clown is farthest from the popcorn? _____

2. Which clown is closest to the popcorn? _____

3. What is the total distance for Curly and Pal? about _____ paper clips

4. What is the total distance for Penny, Tiny, and Pal? about _____ paper clips

Note to the teacher: Each student will need six small paper clips to complete this activity.